2

MEDILAND IS A PLANET SHAPED LIKE THE HUMAN BODY.

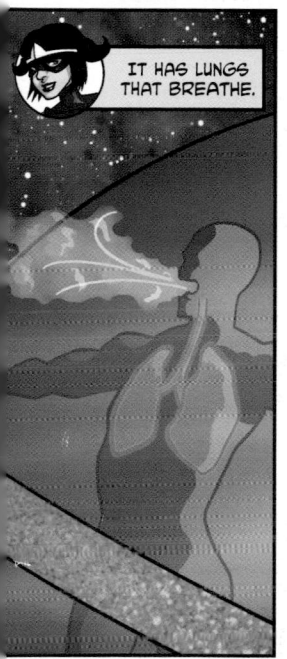

IT HAS LUNGS THAT BREATHE.

A HEART THAT BEATS.

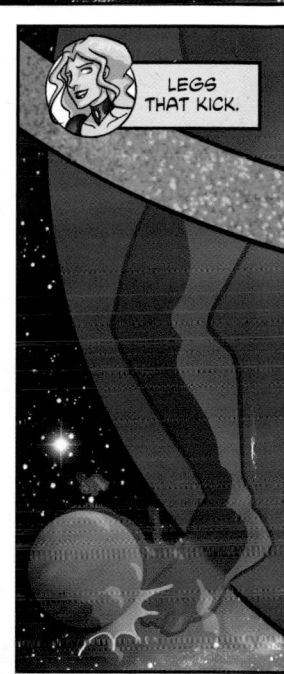

LEGS THAT KICK.

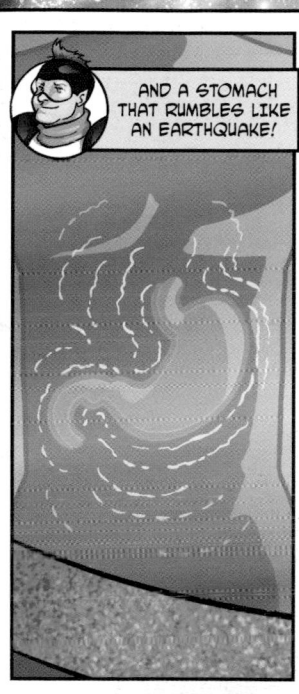

AND A STOMACH THAT RUMBLES LIKE AN EARTHQUAKE!

WE'VE BROUGHT YOU HERE TO TEACH YOU ALL ABOUT *HIV.*

HIV? WHY DIDN'T YOU TELL US?

I WAS ASHAMED. I'VE HEARD WHAT PEOPLE SAY ABOUT HIV.

THERE ARE A LOT OF *RUMOURS* GOING AROUND ABOUT HIV, AND RUMOURS ARE OFTEN *WRONG.*

CLICK

HIV STANDS FOR *HUMAN IMMUNODEFICIENCY VIRUS,* SO FIRST YOU NEED TO UNDERSTAND HOW MOST VIRUSES WORK. TO *THE CELLS!*

8

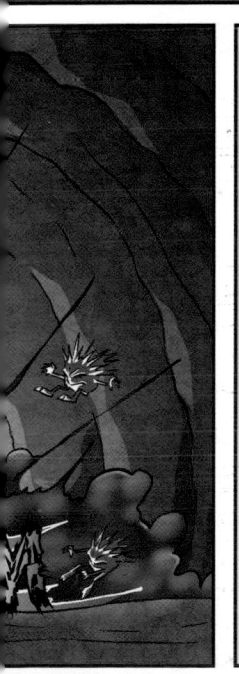

WITHOUT COMMANDERS, EVEN SMALL INFECTIONS CAN HAVE A BIGGER EFFECT AND MAKE YOU VERY SICK! THIS IS WHAT MAKES HIV SO DANGEROUS.
THERE ARE MEDICINES CALLED PROPHYLACTICS WHICH YOU MAY TAKE EVERY DAY TO HELP KEEP YOU FROM GETTING SERIOUS INFECTIONS LIKE PNEUMONIA AND TUBERCULOSIS.

THIS IS TERRIBLE!

HOW DO YOU KNOW IF YOU'VE GOT HIV?
YOU CAN FIND OUT BY HAVING A **BLOOD TEST.**
I'M SORTING THAT OUT NOW. **HOLD ON!**

YOUR DOCTOR OR NURSE WILL TAKE... A **SMALL SAMPLE OF YOUR BLOOD** AND LOOK TO SEE IF THERE'S ANY HIV.
NOOOOO!

THERE ARE DIFFERENT TYPES OF ARVs. SOME STOP HIV MAKING CLONES ONCE IT'S INSIDE THE CELL.
ARE YOU SURE THAT YOU'RE MY ASSISTANT CHEF?
ARV
OF COURSE I AM! HERE, I'VE BROUGHT YOUR NEW MIXING SPOON AS WELL!

ARRGHHH!!!
HAH! GOTCHA!

YOU MIGHT GET **SIDE EFFECTS** FROM YOUR MEDICINES.

THESE ARE THINGS THE MEDICINES DO TO YOU AS WELL AS **STOPPING** HIV FROM MAKING COPIES OF ITSELF, LIKE...

...HEADACHES...

...SKIN RASHES...

...FEELING SICK OR TIRED...

...AND DIARRHOEA.

MOST PEOPLE DON'T HAVE ANY SIDE EFFECTS, BUT IF YOU DO, **DON'T STOP TAKING YOUR MEDICINES!**

TALK TO YOUR DOCTOR OR NURSE STRAIGHT AWAY. THEY CAN TRY **DIFFERENT MEDICINES** THAT WILL SUIT YOU BETTER!

I'M THE BEST AT WHAT I DO!

PFFT, I COULD DO A BETTER JOB. PICK ME!

NO, ME!

NO, ME!

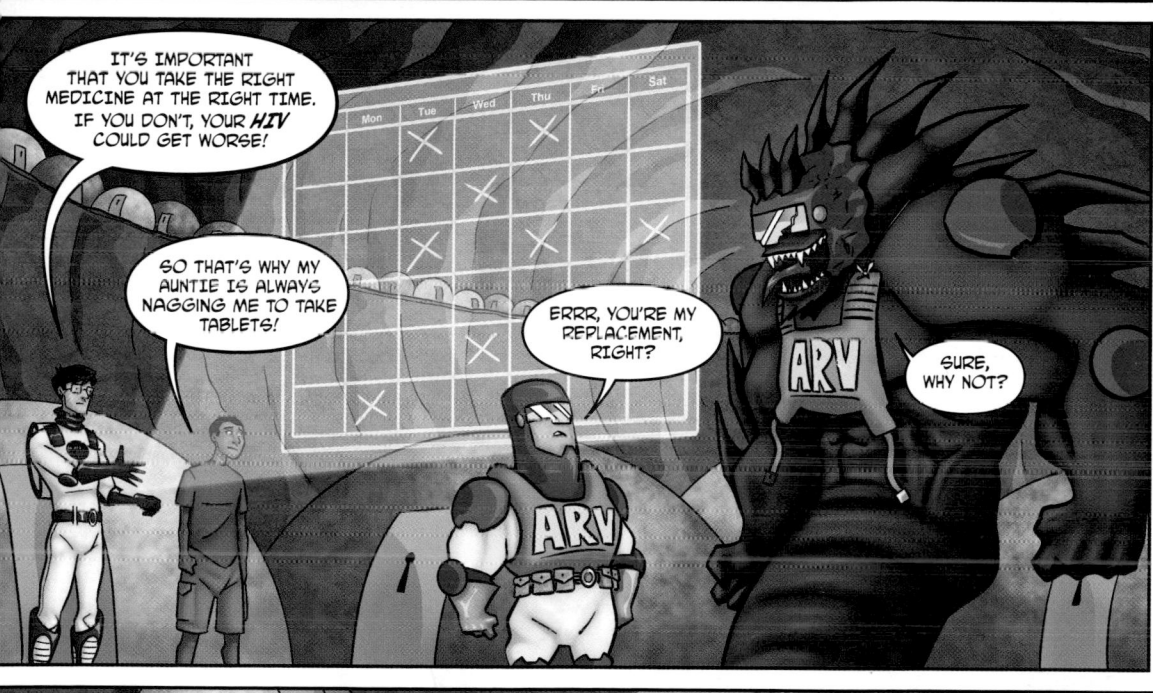

21

HIV LIVES IN YOUR **BLOOD**, SO IT CAN BE PASSED ON IF YOUR BLOOD **MIXES** WITH SOMEONE ELSE'S.

FOR KIDS, THE MOST COMMON WAY TO GET HIV IS TO BE BORN WITH IT.

LOOK OUT—THERE'S A BREAK IN THE SKIN!

LOOK LADS! WE'VE BROKEN THROUGH! CHARGE!

YOU MUST BE CAREFUL AROUND OTHER PEOPLE IF YOU CUT YOURSELF BECAUSE YOUR **BLOOD** CARRIES HIV.

CUTS ALSO LET **GERMS** INTO YOUR BODY, SO MAKE SURE YOU **CLEAN THEM PROPERLY** AND **COVER THEM UP.**

GAH! GET THEM OFF ME! I'LL NEVER BE ABLE TO LIVE A NORMAL LIFE! I'LL HAVE TO STAY AWAY FROM **EVERYONE!**

NOT WHILE YOU HAVE FRIENDS LIKE **US**, YOU WON'T.

THANKS, GUYS!

YOU CAN NEVER *HUG AGAIN!* EVEN SHAKING HANDS IS BAD!

ARGH! GET AWAY FROM ME!

THAT'S ENOUGH FROM YOU! *OUT!*

THERE ARE A LOT OF *MYTHS ABOUT HIV.* YOU *CAN'T* CATCH IT BY *KISSING* OR *HUGGING* ANOTHER PERSON, OR BY *SHAKING HANDS.*

AND YOU CAN'T CATCH IT FROM A *TOILET SEAT.*

BUT IF YOU *HAVE* HIV, IS IT BECAUSE YOU'VE DONE SOMETHING *WRONG?* THAT YOU *DESERVE* IT?

NOT AT ALL! IF YOU HAVE *HIV,* IT DOESN'T MEAN YOU'RE A *BAD PERSON.* ANYBODY CAN CATCH IT!

NO ONE CAN TELL BY *LOOKING* AT YOU THAT YOU HAVE HIV.

IF YOU KEEP TAKING YOUR *MEDICATION* YOU CAN LIVE A NORMAL LIFE.

THERE'S NOTHING TO STOP YOU GOING TO *UNIVERSITY* OR HAVING A *JOB* AND *FAMILY* ONE DAY, JUST LIKE OTHER PEOPLE.

YOUR MEDICINES ARE JUST ONE WAY OF MAKING SURE YOU STAY **WELL**. THERE ARE LOTS OF ***OTHER THINGS*** YOU CAN DO TOO.
REMEMBER, ***YOU'RE*** IN CHARGE OF YOUR HIV, NOT THE OTHER WAY AROUND.
YEAH! ***FEEL THE BURN!***
GETTING REGULAR EXERCISE IS REALLY HELPFUL BECAUSE IT KEEPS YOU HEALTHY.
YOUR DOCTORS AND NURSES CAN GIVE YOU ADVICE ON ALL THE DIFFERENT FOODS YOU CAN EAT TO STAY HEALTHY.
YEAH, BUT ALL OF THEM AT THE SAME TIME? EURGH!
IF YOU SEE THEM REGULARLY, THEY CAN ALSO CHECK UP ON HOW YOU'RE DOING!

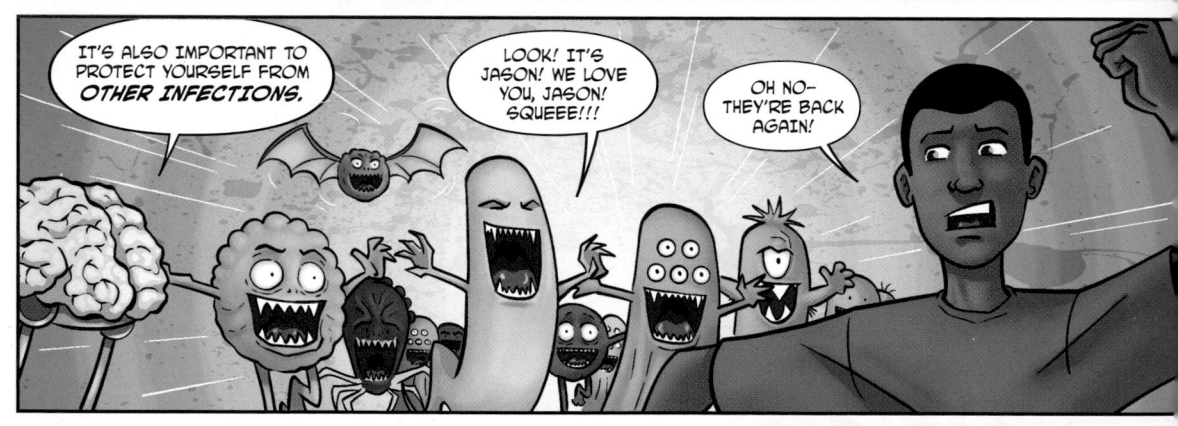

IN THE MOUTH...

LOOK, THERE ARE SOME GERMS TRYING TO INVADE!

THAT'S WHY *WASHING YOUR HANDS* IS SO IMPORTANT.

OF COURSE, I DON'T *HAVE* HANDS, SO I WOULDN'T KNOW.

I'VE GOT THIS.

YOU SHOULD WASH YOUR HANDS BEFORE AND AFTER *PREPARING OR EATING FOOD*...

...IF YOU'VE BEEN SOMEWHERE *CROWDED*...

...AFTER GOING TO THE *TOILET*...

...OR AFTER *TOUCHING ANIMALS.*

WAIT—WHAT EXACTLY DO YOU THINK I AM? *STOP PETTING ME!*

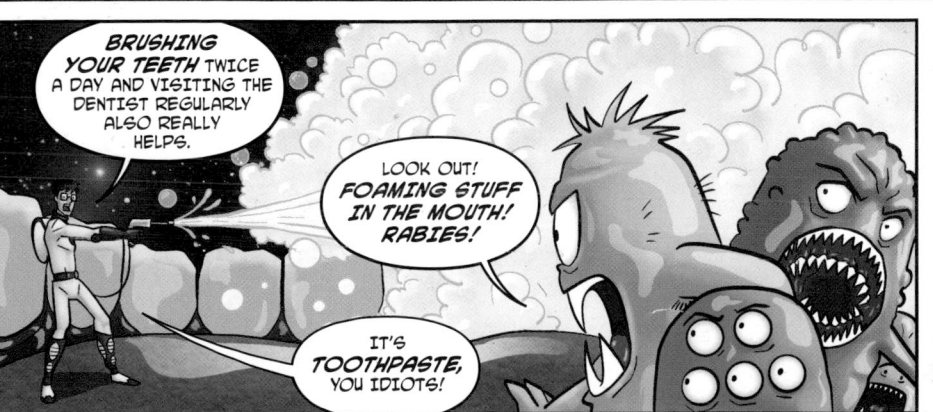

BRUSHING YOUR TEETH TWICE A DAY AND VISITING THE DENTIST ALSO REALLY HELPS.

LOOK OUT! *FOAMING STUFF IN THE MOUTH! RABIES!*

IT'S *TOOTHPASTE,* YOU IDIOTS!

I THINK IT'S TIME TO *HEAD FOR HOME!*

CLICK

IT CAN BE A GOOD IDEA TO TELL YOUR TRUSTED **FRIENDS, FAMILY AND TEACHERS** TOO, SO THEY CAN HELP.

IT'S YOUR CHOICE **WHO** YOU TELL AND **WHEN** YOU TELL THEM.

THE MEDIKIDZ ARE RIGHT. YOU **SHOULD** TELL YOUR TRUSTED FRIENDS, LIKE **I** SHOULD.

I HAVE HIV TOO. I TAKE TABLETS EVERY DAY...

...AND FOR YEARS I'VE FELT **SCARED** AND **ALONE.**

SO **THAT'S** WHY YOU WERE QUIET EARLIER! YOU SHOULD HAVE **TOLD US!** WE COULD HAVE HELPED YOU!

BUT NOW WE **ALL** KNOW, WE CAN **SUPPORT EACH OTHER!** LOOK OUT FOR ONE ANOTHER!

THANKS GUYS—AND JASON, I'LL **ALWAYS** HAVE YOUR BACK, BRO.

SO, DO YOU THINK YOU UNDERSTAND HIV?

YEAH, HIV IS A *VIRUS* THAT ATTACKS *CD4 CELLS*.

THIS MEANS THEY CAN'T DO THEIR JOB.

IF THAT HAPPENS, THE *IMMUNE SYSTEM ARMY* DOESN'T GET ORDERS TO START *FIGHTING*, SO THERE'S *NOTHING* PROTECTING MY BODY.

I COULD GET REALLY SICK WITH *OPPORTUNISTIC INFECTIONS*.

LUCKILY THERE ARE *PROPHYLACTIC MEDICINES* TO HELP PREVENT ME GETTING INFECTIONS...

...AND *ARV MEDICINES* TO STOP HIV MAKING CLONES.